My Toy Box Is Heavy

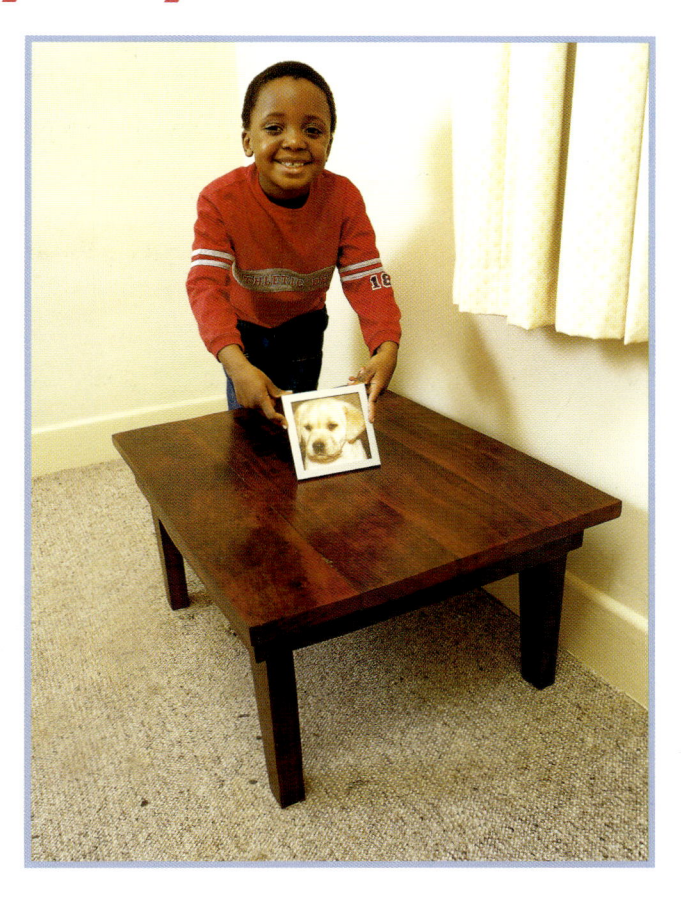

Constable Daniel Woodall Library

George Wong

Tom's Room

This is my new bedroom. Mom helps me move my things into my room.

My table is **heavy**.
Mom moves it into my room.

My picture is **light**.
I move it into my room.

My chair is **heavy**.
Mom moves it into my room.

My pillow is **light**.
I move it into my room.

My bookcase is **heavy**.
Mom moves it into my room.

My book is **light**.
I move it into my room.

My toy box is **heavy**.
Mom moves it into my room.

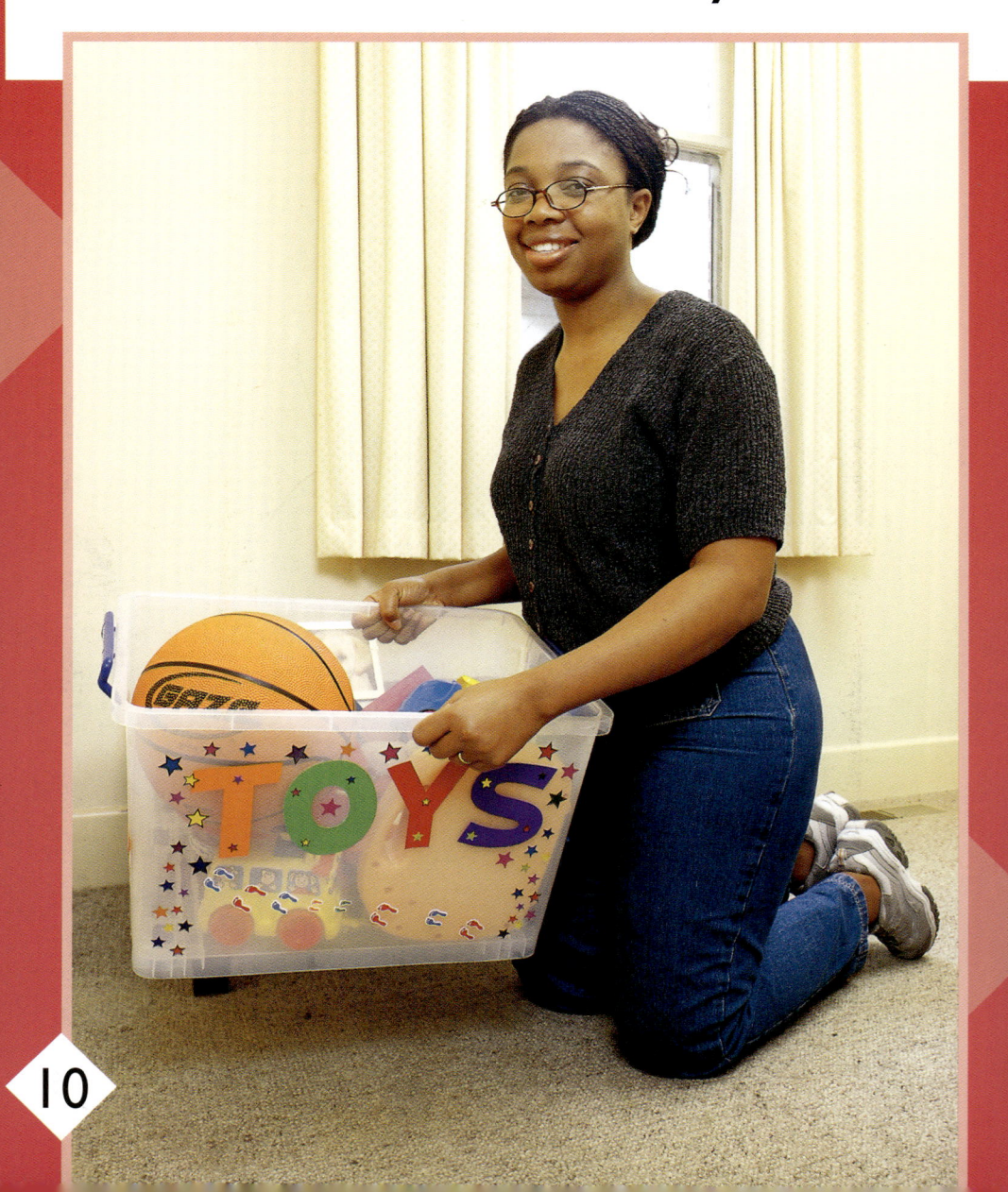

My teddy bear is **light**.
I move it into my room.

Heavy Light

12